THE GO GETTER

(A STORY THAT TELLS YOU HOW TO BE ONE)

PETER B KYNE

SANAGE
PUBLISHING HOUSE

Paperback: 978-939492438-3

Printed by: Manipal Technologies Limited, Manipal

Sanage Publishing House LLP
Mumbai, India

sanagepublishing@gmail.com

Peter B Kyne was a novelist and short story writer from The United States. Many of his works were adapted into screenplays. His book **The Go-Getter** at one time became like a bible for salesmen, businessmen and entrepreneurs, inspiring them to achieve more.

CONTENTS

DEDICATION

THIS LITTLE BOOK IS DEDICATED TO THE MEMORY OF MY DEAD CHIEF, BRIGADIER-GENERAL LEROY S. LYON, SOMETIME COMMANDER OF THE 65TH FIELD ARTILLERY BRIGADE, 40TH DIVISION, UNITED STATES ARMY.

HE PRACTICED AND PREACHED A RELIGION OF LOYALTY TO THE COUNTRY AND THE APPOINTED TASK, WHATEVER IT MIGHT BE.

Chapter I

Mr. Alden P. Ricks, known in Pacific Coast wholesale lumber and shipping circles as Cappy Ricks, had more troubles than a hen with ducklings. He remarked as much to Mr. Skinner, president and general manager of the Ricks Logging & Lumbering Company, the corporate entity which represented Cappy's vast lumber interests; and he fairly barked the information at Captain Matt Peasley, his son-in-law and also president and manager of the Blue Star Navigation Company, another corporate entity which represented the Ricks interest in the American mercantile marine.

Mr. Skinner received this information in silence. He was not related to Cappy Ricks. But Matt Peasley sat down, crossed his legs and matched glares with his mercurial father-in-law.

"You have troubles!" he jeered, with emphasis on the pronoun. "Have you got a misery in your back, or is Herbert Hoover the wrong man for Secretary of Commerce?"

"Stow your sarcasm, young feller," Cappy shrilled. "You know dad-blamed well it isn't a question of health or politics. It's the fact that in my old age I find myself totally surrounded by the choicest aggregation of mental duds since Ajax defied the lightning."

"Meaning whom?"

"You and Skinner."

"Why, what have we done?"

"You argued me into taking on the management of twenty-five of those infernal Shipping Board freighters, and no sooner do we have them allocated to us than a near panic hits the country, freight rates go to glory, marine engineers go on strike and every infernal young whelp we send out to take charge of one of our offices in the Orient promptly gets the swelled head and thinks he's divinely ordained to drink up all the synthetic Scotch whiskey manufactured in Japan for the benefit of thirsty Americans. In my old age you two have forced us into the position of having to fire folks by cable. Why? Because we're breaking into a game that can't be played on the home grounds. A lot of our business is so far away we can't control it."

Matt Peasley levelled an accusing finger at Cappy Ricks. "We never argued you into taking over the management of those Shipping Board boats. We argued me into it. I'm the goat. You have nothing to do with it. You retired ten years ago. All the troubles in the marine end of this shop belong on my capable shoulders, old settler."

"Theoretically--yes. Actually--no. I hope you do not expect me to abandon mental as well as physical effort. Great Wampus Cats! Am I to be denied a sentimental interest in matters where I have a controlling financial interest? I admit you two boys are running my affairs and ordinarily you run them rather well, but..but..ahem! Harumph-h-h! What's the matter with you, Matt? And you, also, Skinner? If Matt makes a mistake, it's your job to remind him of it before the results manifest themselves, is it not? And vice versa. Have you two boobs lost your ability to judge men, or did you ever have such ability?"

"You're referring to Henderson, of the Shanghai office, I dare say," Mr. Skinner cut in.

"I am, Skinner. And I'm here to remind you that if we'd stuck to our own game, which is coast-wise shipping, and had left the trans-Pacific field with its general cargoes to others, we wouldn't have any Shanghai office at this moment and we would not be pestered by the

Henderson's of this world."

"He's the best lumber salesman we've ever had," Mr. Skinner defended. "I had every hope that he would send us orders for many a cargo for Asiatic delivery."

"And he had gone through every job in this office, from office boy to sales manager in the lumber department and from freight clerk to passenger agent in the navigation company," Matt Peasley supplemented.

"I admit all of that. But did you consult me when you decided to send him out to China on his own?"

"Of course not. I'm boss of the Blue Star Navigation Company, am I not? The man was in charge of the Shanghai office before you ever opened your mouth to discharge your cargo of free advice."

"I told you then that Henderson wouldn't make good, didn't I?"

"You did."

"And now I have an opportunity to tell you the little tale you didn't give me an opportunity to tell you before you sent him out. Henderson was a good man, a crackerjack man when he had a better man over him. But I've been twenty years reducing a tendency on the part of that fellow's head to bust his hatband. And now he's gone south with a hundred and thirty thousand taels of our Shanghai bank account."

"Permit me to remind you, Mr. Ricks," Mr. Skinner cut in coldly, "that he was bonded to the extent of a quarter of a million dollars."

"Not a peep out of you, Skinner. Not a peep. Permit me to remind you that I'm the little genius who placed that insurance unknown to you and Matt. And I recall now that I was reminded by you, Matthew, my son, that I had retired ten years ago and please, would I quit interfering in the internal administration of your office."

"Well, I must admit your far-sightedness in that instance will keep the Shanghai office out of the red ink this year," Matt Peasley replied. "However, we face this situation, Cappy. Henderson has drunk and gambled and signed chits in excess of his salary. He hasn't attended to business, and he's capped his inefficiency by absconding with our bank account. We couldn't foresee that. When we send a man out to the Orient to be our manager there, we have to trust him all the way or not at all. So, there is no use weeping over spilled milk, Cappy. Our job is to select a successor to Henderson and send him out to Shanghai on the next boat."

"Oh, very well, Matt," Cappy replied magnanimously, "I'll not rub it into you. I suppose I'm far from generous, bawling you out like this. Perhaps, when you're my age and have a lot of mental and moral cripples nip you and draw blood as often as they've drawn it on me, you'll be a better judge than I of men worthy of the weight of responsibility. Skinner, have you got a candidate for this job?"

"I regret to say, sir, I have not. All of the men in my department are quite young, too young for the responsibility."

"What do you mean, young?" Cappy blazed.

"Well, the only man I would consider for the job is Andrews and he is too young about thirty, I should say."

"About thirty, eh? Strikes me you were about twenty-eight when I threw ten thousand a year at you in actual cash, and a couple of million dollars' worth of responsibility."

"Yes sir, but then Andrews has never been tested...."

"Skinner," Cappy interrupted in his most awful voice, "it's a constant source of amazement to me why I refrain from firing you. You say Andrews has never been tested. Why hasn't he been tested? Why are we maintaining untested material in this shop, anyhow? Eh? Answer me that. Tut, tut, tut! Not a peep out of you, sir. If you had done your Christian duty, you would have taken a year's vacation when lumber was selling itself in 1919 and 1920, and you would have left Andrews sitting in at your desk to see the sort of stuff he's made of."

"It's a mighty lucky thing I didn't go away for a year," Skinner protested respectfully, "because the market broke like that and if you don't think we have to hustle to sell sufficient lumber to keep our own ships busy freighting it"

"Skinner, how dare you contradict me? How old was Matt Peasley when I turned over the Blue Star Navigation Company to him, lock, stock, and barrel? Why, he wasn't twenty-six years old. Skinner, you're a dodo! The killjoys like you who have straddled the neck of industry and throttled it with absurd theories that a man's back must be bent like an oxbow and his locks snowy white before he can be entrusted with responsibility and a living wage, have caused all of our wars and strikes. This is a young man's world, Skinner, and don't you ever forget it. The go-getters of this world are under thirty years of age. Matt," he concluded, turning to his son-in-law, "what do you think of Andrews for that Shanghai job?"

"I think he'll do."

"Why do you think he'll do?"

"Because he ought to do. He's been with us long enough to have acquired sufficient experience to enable him"

"Has he acquired the courage to tackle the job, Matt?" Cappy interrupted. "That's more important than this dogged experience you and Skinner prate so much about."

"I know nothing of his courage. I assume that he has force and initiative. I know he has a pleasing personality."

"Well, before we send him out, we ought to know whether or no he has force and initiative."

"Then," quote Matt Peasley, rising, "I wash my hands of the job of selecting Henderson's successor. You've butted in, so I suggest you name the lucky man."

"Yes, indeed," Skinner agreed. "I'm sure it's quite beyond my poor abilities to uncover Andrews' force and initiative on such notice. He does possess sufficient force and initiative for his present job, but"

"But will he possess force and initiative when he has to make a quick decision six thousand miles from expert advice, and stand or fall by that decision? That's what we want to know, Skinner."

"I suggest, sir," Mr. Skinner replied with chill politeness, "that you conduct the examination."

"I accept the nomination, Skinner. By the Holy Pink-toed Prophet! The next man we send out to that Shanghai office is going to be a go-getter. We've had three managers go rotten on us and that's three too many."

And without further ado, Cappy swung his aged legs up on to his desk and slid down in his swivel chair until he rested on his spine. His head sank on his breast, and he closed his eyes.

"He's framing the examination for Andrews," Matt Peasley whispered, as he and Skinner made their exits.

Chapter II

The President emeritus of the Ricks' interests was not destined to uninterrupted cogitation, however. Within ten minutes his private exchange operator called him to the telephone.

"What is it?" Cappy yelled into the transmitter.

"There is a young man in the general office. His name is Mr. William E. Peck, and he desires to see you personally."

Cappy sighed. "Very well," he replied. "Have him shown in."

Almost immediately the office boy ushered Mr. Peck into Cappy's presence. The moment he was fairly inside the door the visitor halted, came easily and naturally to "attention" and bowed respectfully, while the cool glance of his keen blue eyes held steadily the autocrat of the Blue Star Navigation Company.

"Mr. Ricks, Peck is my name, sir William E. Peck. Thank you, sir, for acceding to my request for an interview."

"Ahem! Hum-m-m!" Cappy looked belligerent. "Sit down, Mr. Peck."

Mr. Peck sat down, but as he crossed to the chair beside Cappy's desk, the old gentleman noticed that his visitor walked with a slight limp, and that his left forearm had been amputated halfway to the elbow. To the observant Cappy, the American Legion button in Mr. Peck's lapel told the story.

"Well, Mr. Peck," he queried gently, "what can I do for you?"

"I've called for my job," the veteran replied briefly.

"By the Holy Pink-toed Prophet!" Cappy ejaculated, "you say that like a man who doesn't expect to be refused."

"Quite right, sir. I do not anticipate a refusal."

"Why?"

Mr. William E. Peck's engaging but somewhat plain features rippled into the most compelling smile Cappy Ricks had ever seen. "I am a salesman, Mr. Ricks," he replied. "I know that statement to be true because I have demonstrated, over a period of five years, that I can sell my share of anything that has a hockable value. I have always found, however, that before proceeding to sell goods I had to sell the manufacturer of those goods something, to wit myself! I am about to sell myself to you."

"Son," said Cappy smilingly, "you win. You've sold me already. When did they sell you a membership in the military forces of the United States of America?"

"On the morning of April 7th, 1917, sir."

"That clinches our sale. I soldiered with the Knights of Columbus at Camp Kearny myself, but when they refused to let me go abroad with my division my heart was broken, so I went over the hill."

That little touch of the language of the line appeared to warm Mr. Peck's heart considerably, establishing at once a free masonry between them.

"I was with the Portland Lumber Company, selling lumber in the Middle West before the war," he explained. "Uncle Sam gave me my sheepskin at Letter-man General Hospital last week, with half disability on my ten thousand dollars' worth of government insurance. Whittling my wing was a mere trifle, but my broken leg was a long-time mending, and now it's shorter than it really ought to be. And I developed pneumonia with influenza, and they found some T.B. indications after that. I've been at the government tuberculosis hospital at Fort Bayard, New Mexico, for a year. However, what's left of me is certified to be sound. I've got five inches chest expansion and I feel fine."

"Not at all blue or discouraged?" Cappy hazarded.

"Oh, I got off easy, Mr. Ricks. I have my head left and my right arm. I can think and I can write, and even if one of my wheels is flat, I can hike longer and faster after an order than most. Got a job for me, Mr. Ricks?"

"No, I haven't, Mr. Peck. I'm out of it, you know. Retired ten years ago. This office is merely a headquarters for social frivolity, a place to get my mail and mill over the gossip of the street. Our Mr. Skinner is the chap you should see."

"I have seen Mr. Skinner, sir," the erstwhile warrior replied, "but he wasn't very sympathetic. I think he jumped to the conclusion that I was attempting to trade him my empty sleeve. He informed me that there wasn't sufficient business to keep his present staff of salesmen busy, so then I told him I'd take anything, from stenographer up. I'm the champion one-handed typist of the United States Army. I can tally lumber and bill it. I can keep books and answer the telephone."

"No encouragement, eh?"

"No, sir."

"Well, now, son," Cappy informed his cheerful visitor confidentially, "you take my tip and see my son-in-law, Captain Peasley. He's high, low and jack-in-the-game in the shipping end of our business."

"I have also interviewed Captain Peasley. He was very kind. He said he felt that he owed me a job, but business is so bad he couldn't make a place for me. He told me he is now carrying a dozen ex-service men merely because he hasn't the heart to let them go. I believe him."

"Well, my dear boy, my dear young friend! Why do you come to me?"

"Because" Mr. Peck replied smilingly, "I want you to go over their heads and give me a job. I don't care a hoot what it is, provided I can do it. If I can do it, I'll do it better than it was ever done before, and if I can't do that, I'll quit to save you the embarrassment of firing me. I'm not an object of charity, but I'm scarcely the man I used to be and I'm four years behind the procession and have to catch up. I have the best of references"

"I see you have," Cappy cut in blandly, and pressed the push-button on his desk. Mr. Skinner entered. He glanced disapprovingly at William E. Peck and then turned inquiring eyes toward Cappy Ricks.

"Skinner, dear boy," Cappy purred amiably, "I've been thinking over the proposition to send Andrews out to the Shanghai office, and I've come to this conclusion. We'll have to take a chance. At the present time that office is in charge of a stenographer, and we've got to get a manager on the job without further loss of time. So, I'll tell you what we'll do. We'll send Andrews out on the next boat but inform him that his position is temporary. Then if he doesn't make good out there, we can take him back into this office, where he is a most valuable man. Meanwhile ahem! Hum.m.m! Harumph! meanwhile, you'd oblige me greatly, Skinner, my dear boy, if you would consent to take this young man into your office and give him a good work-out to see the stuff he's made of. As a favour to me, Skinner, my dear boy, as a favour to me."

Mr. Skinner, in the language of the sporting world, was down for the count and knew it. Young Mr. Peck knew it too, and smiled graciously upon the general manager, for young Mr. Peck had been in the army, where one of the first great lessons to be assimilated is this: that the commanding general's request is always tantamount to an order.

"Very well, sir," Mr. Skinner replied coldly. "Have you arranged the compensation to be given Mr. Peck?"

Cappy threw up a deprecating hand. "That detail is entirely up to you,

Skinner. Far be it from me to interfere in the internal administration of your department. Naturally you will pay Mr. Peck what he is worth and not a cent more." He turned to the triumphant Peck. "Now, you listen to me, young feller. If you think you're slipping gracefully into a good thing, disabuse your mind of that impression right now. You'll step right up to the plate, my son, and you'll hit the ball fairly on the nose, and you'll do it early and often. The first time you tip a foul, you'll be warned. The second time you do it you'll get a month's lay-off to think it over, and the third time you'll be out for keeps. Do I make myself clear?"

"You do, sir," Mr. Peck declared happily. "All I ask is fighting room and I'll hack my way into Mr. Skinner's heart. Thank you, Mr. Skinner, for consenting to take me on. I appreciate your action very, very much and shall endeavour to be worthy of your confidence."

"Young scoundrel! In-fer-nal young scoundrel!" Cappy murmured to himself. "He has a sense of humour, thank God! Ah, poor old narrow-gauge Skinner! If that fellow ever gets a new or unconventional thought in his stodgy head, it'll kill him overnight. He's hopping mad right now, because he can't say a word in his own defence, but if he doesn't make hell look like a summer holiday for Mr. Bill Peck, I'm due to be mercifully chloroformed. Good Lord, how empty life would be if I couldn't butt in and raise a little riot every once in so often."

Young Mr. Peck had risen and was standing at attention. "When do I report for duty, sir?" he queried of Mr. Skinner.

"Whenever you're ready," Skinner retorted with a wintry smile. Mr. Peck glanced at a cheap wristwatch. "It's twelve o'clock now," he soliloquized aloud. "I'll pop out, wrap myself around some rations and report on the job at one P.M. I might just as well knock out half a day's pay." He glanced at Cappy Ricks and quoted:

"Count that day lost whose low descending sun

Finds prices shot to glory and business done for fun."

Unable to maintain his composure in the face of such levity during office hours, Mr. Skinner withdrew, still wrapped in his sub-Antarctic dignity. As the door closed behind him, Mr. Peck's eyebrows went up in a manner indicative of apprehension.

"I'm off to a bad start, Mr. Ricks," he opined.

"You only asked for a start," Cappy piped back at him. "I didn't guarantee you a good start, and I wouldn't because I can't. I can only drive Skinner and Matt Peasley so far and no farther. There's always a point at which I quit...er...ah..William."

"More familiarly known as Bill Peck, sir."

"Very well, Bill." Cappy slid out to the edge of his chair and peered at Bill Peck balefully over the top of his spectacles. "I'll have my eye on you, young feller," he shrilled. "I freely acknowledge our indebtedness to you, but the day you get the notion in your head that this office is an old soldiers' home" He paused thoughtfully. "I wonder what Skinner will pay you?" he mused. "Oh, well," he continued, whatever it is, take it and say nothing and when the moment is propitious and provided you've earned it, I'll intercede with the danged old relic and get you a raise."

"Thank you very much, sir. You are most kind. Good-day, sir."

And Bill Peck picked up his hat and limped out of The Presence. Scarcely had the door closed behind him than Mr. Skinner re-entered Cappy Ricks' lair. He opened his mouth to speak, but Cappy silenced him with an imperious finger.

"Not a peep out of you, Skinner, my dear boy," he chirped amiably. "I know exactly what you're going to say, and I admit your right to say it, but as ahem! Harumph-h-h!..now, Skinner, listen to reason. How the devil could you have the heart to reject that crippled ex-soldier? There he stood on one sound leg, with his sleeve tucked into his coat pocket and on his homely face the grin of an unwhipped, unbeatable man. But you blast your cold, unfeeling soul, Skinner! looked him in the eye and turned him down like a drunkard turns down near-beer. Skinner, how could you do it?"

Undaunted by Cappy's admonitory finger, Mr. Skinner struck a distinctly defiant attitude.

"There is no sentiment in business," he replied angrily. "A week ago, last Thursday the local posts of the American Legion commenced their organized drive for jobs for their crippled and unemployed comrades, and within three days you've sawed off two hundred and nine such jobs on the various corporations that you control. The gang you shipped up to the mill in Washington has already applied for a charter for a new post to be known as Cappy Ricks Post No. 534. And you had experienced men discharged to make room for these ex-soldiers."

"You bet I did," Cappy yelled triumphantly. "It's always Old Home Week in every logging camp and saw-mill in the Northwest for I.W.W.'s and revolutionary communists. I'm sick of their unauthorized strikes and sabotage, and by the Holy Pink-Toed Prophet, Cappy Ricks Post. No. 534, American Legion, is the only sort of back-fire I can think of to put the Wobblies on the run."

"Every office and ship and retail yard could be run by a first-sergeant," Skinner complained. "I'm thinking of having reveille and retreat and bugle calls and Saturday morning inspections. I tell you, sir, the Ricks interests have absorbed all the old soldiers possible and at the present moment those interests are overflowing with glory. What we want are workers, not talkers. These ex-soldiers spend too much time fighting their battles over again."

"Well, Comrade Peck is the last one I'll ask you to absorb, Skinner," Cappy promised contritely. "Ever read Kipling's Barrack Room Ballads, Skinner?"

"I have no time to read," Mr. Skinner protested.

"Go up town this minute and buy a copy and read one ballad entitled 'Tommy,'" Cappy barked. "For the good of your immortal soul," he added.

"Well, Comrade Peck doesn't make a hit with me, Mr. Ricks. He applied to me for a job, and I gave him his answer. Then he went to Captain Matt and was refused, so, just to demonstrate his bad taste, he went over our heads and induced you to pitchfork him into a job. He'll curse the day he was inspired to do that."

"Skinner! Skinner! Look me in the eye! Do you know why I asked you to take on Bill Peck?"

"I do. Because you're too tender-hearted for your own good."

"You unimaginative dunderhead! You are jabbering jackdaw! How could I reject a boy who simply would not be rejected? Why, I'll bet a ripe peach that Bill Peck was one of the doggondest finest soldiers you ever saw? He carries his objective. He sized you up just like that, Skinner. He declined to permit you to block him. Skinner, that Peck person has been opposed by experts. Yes, sir experts! What kind of a job are you going to give him, Skinner, my dear boy?"

"Andrews' job, of course."

"Oh, yes, I forgot. Skinner, dear boy, haven't we got about half a million feet of skunk spruce to saw off on somebody?" Mr. Skinner nodded and Cappy continued with all the naïve eagerness of one who has just made a marvellous discovery, which he is confident will revolutionize science. "Give him that stinking stuff to peddle, Skinner, and if you can dig up a couple of dozen carloads of red fir or bull pine in transit, or some short or odd-length stock, or some larch ceiling or flooring, or some hemlock random stock in fact, anything the trade doesn't want as a gift, you get me, don't you, Skinner?"

Mr. Skinner smiled his swordfish smile. "And if he fails to make good au revoir, eh?"

"Yes, I suppose so, although I hate to think about it. On the other hand, if he makes good, he's to have Andrews' salary. We must be fair, Skinner. Whatever our faults we must always be fair." He rose and patted the general manager's lean shoulder. "There, there, Skinner, my boy. Forgive me if I've been a trifle..ah..ahem! precipitate and.. er..harumph.h.h! Skinner, if you put a prohibitive price on that skunk fir, by the Holy Pink-toed Prophet, I'll fire you! Be fair, boy, be fair. No dirty work, Skinner. Remember, Comrade Peck has half of his left forearm buried in France."

Chapter III

At twelve-thirty, as Cappy was hurrying up California Street to luncheon at the Commercial Club, he met Bill Peck limping down the sidewalk. The ex-soldier stopped him and handed him a card.

"What do you think of that, sir?" he queried. "Isn't it a neat business card?"

Cappy read:

RICKS LUMBER & LOGGING COMPANY
Lumber and its products
248 California St.
San Francisco.

Represented by
William E. Peck

If you can drive nails in it, we have it!

Cappy Ricks ran a speculative thumb over Comrade Peck's business card. It was engraved. And copper plates or steel dies are not made in half an hour!

"By the Twelve Ragged Apostles!" This was Cappy's most terrible oath and he never employed it unless rocked to his very foundations. "Bill, as one bandit to another come clean. When did you first make up your mind to go to work for us?"

"A week ago," Comrade Peck replied blandly.

"And what was your grade when Kaiser Bill went A.W.O.L.?"

"I was a buck."

"I don't believe you. Didn't anybody ever offer you something better?"

"Frequently. However, if I had accepted, I would have had to resign the nicest job I ever had. There wasn't much money in it, but it was filled with excitement and interesting experiments. I used to disguise myself as a Christmas tree or a box car and pick off German sharpshooters. I was known as Peck's Bad Boy. I was often tempted to quit, but whenever I'd reflect on the number of American lives I was saving daily, a commission was just a scrap of paper to me."

"If you'd ever started in any other branch of the service, you'd have run John J. Pershing down to lance corporal. Bill, listen! Have you ever had any experience selling skunk spruce?"

Comrade Peck was plainly puzzled. He shook his head. "What sort of stock is it?" he asked.

"Humboldt County, California, spruce, and it's coarse and stringy and wet and heavy and smells just like a skunk directly after using. I'm afraid Skinner's going to start you at the bottom and skunk spruce is it.

"Can you drive nails in it, Mr. Ricks?"

"Oh, yes."

"Does anybody ever buy skunk spruce, sir?"

"Oh, occasionally one of our bright young men digs up a half-wit who's willing to try anything once. Otherwise, of course, we would not continue to manufacture it. Fortunately, Bill, we have very little of it, but whenever our woods boss runs across a good tree, he hasn't the heart to leave it standing, and as a result, we always have enough skunk spruce on hand to keep our salesmen humble."

"I can sell anything at a price," Comrade Peck replied unconcernedly, and continued on his way back to the office.

Chapter IV

For two months Cappy Ricks saw nothing of Bill Peck. That enterprising veteran had been sent out into the Utah, Arizona, New Mexico, and Texas territory the moment he had familiarized himself with the numerous details regarding freight rates, weights, and the mills he represented, all things which a salesman should be familiar with before he starts out on the road. From Salt Lake City he wired an order for two carloads of larch rustic and in Ogden he managed to inveigle a retail yard with which Mr. Skinner had been trying to do business for years, into sampling a carload of skunk spruce boards, random lengths, and grades, at a dollar above the price given him by Skinner. In Arizona he worked up some new business in mining timbers, but it was not until he got into the heart of Texas that Comrade Peck really commenced to demonstrate his selling ability. Standard oil derricks were his specialty, and he shot the orders in so fast that Mr. Skinner was forced to wire him for mercy and instruct him to devote his talent to the disposal of cedar shingles and siding, Douglas fir and redwood. Eventually he completed his circle and worked his way home, via Los Angeles, pausing however, in the San Joaquin Valley to sell two more carloads of skunk spruce. When this order was wired in, Mr. Skinner came to Cappy Ricks with the telegram.

"Well, I must admit Comrade Peck can sell lumber," he announced grudgingly. "He has secured five new accounts and here is an order for two more carloads of skunk spruce. I'll have to raise his salary about the first of the year.

"My dear Skinner, why the devil wait until the first of the year? Your pernicious habit of deferring the inevitable parting with money has cost us the services of more than one good man. You know you have to raise Comrade Peck's salary sooner or later, so why not do it now and smile like a dentifrice advertisement while you're doing it? Comrade Peck will feel a whole lot better as a result, and who knows? He may conclude you're a human being, after all, and learn to love you?"

"Very well, sir. I'll give him the same salary Andrews was getting before Peck took over his territory."

"Skinner, you make it impossible for me to refrain from showing you who's boss around here. He's better than Andrews, isn't he?"

"I think he is, sir."

"Well then, for the love of a square deal, pay him more and pay it to him from the first day he went to work. Get out. You make me nervous. By the way, how is Andrews getting along in his Shanghai job?"

"He's helping the cable company pay its income tax. Cables about three times a week on matters he should decide for himself. Matt Peasley is disgusted with him."

"Ah! Well, I'm not disappointed. And I suppose Matt will be in here before long to remind me that I was the bright boy who picked Andrews for the job. Well, I did, but I call upon you to remember. Skinner, when I'm assailed, that Andrews' appointment was temporary."

"Yes, sir, it was."

"Well, I suppose I'll have to cast about for his successor and beat Matt out of his cheap 'I told you so' triumph. I think Comrade Peck has some of the earmarks of a good manager for our Shanghai office, but I'll have to test him a little further." He looked up humorously at Mr.

Skinner. "Skinner, my dear boy," he continued, "I'm going to have him deliver a blue vase."

Mr. Skinner's cold features actually glowed. "Well, tip the chief of police and the proprietor of the store off this time and save yourself some money," he warned Cappy. He walked to the window and looked down into California Street. He continued to smile.

"Yes," Cappy continued dreamily, "I think I shall give him the thirty-third degree. You'll agree with me, Skinner, that if he delivers the blue vase, he'll be worth ten thousand dollars a year as our Oriental manager?"

"I'll say he will," Mr. Skinner replied slangily.

"Very well, then. Arrange matters, Skinner, so that he will be available for me at one o'clock, a week from Sunday. I'll attend to the other details."

Mr. Skinner nodded. He was still chuckling when he departed for his own office.

Chapter V

A week from the succeeding Saturday, Mr. Skinner did not come down to the office, but a telephone message from his home informed the chief clerk that Mr. Skinner was at home and somewhat indisposed. The chief clerk was to advise Mr. Peck that he, Mr. Skinner, had contemplated having a conference with the latter that day, but that his indisposition would prevent this. Mr. Skinner hoped to be feeling much better tomorrow, and since he was very desirous of a conference with Mr. Peck before the latter should depart on his next selling pilgrimage, on Monday, would Mr. Peck be good enough to call at Mr. Skinner's house at one o'clock Sunday afternoon? Mr. Peck sent back word that he would be there at the appointed time and was rewarded with Mr. Skinner's thanks, via the chief clerk.

Promptly at one o'clock the following day, Bill Peck reported at the general manager's house. He found Mr. Skinner in bed, reading the paper, and looking surprisingly well. He trusted Mr. Skinner felt better than he looked. Mr. Skinner did, and at once entered into a discussion of the new customers, other prospects he particularly desired Mr. Peck to approach, new business to be investigated, and further details without end. And in the midst of this conference Cappy Riggs telephoned.

A portable telephone stood on a commode beside Mr. Skinner's bed, so the latter answered immediately. Comrade Peck watched Skinner listen attentively for fully two minutes, then heard him say:

"Mr. Ricks, I'm terribly sorry. I'd love to do this errand for you, but really, I'm under the weather. In fact, I'm in bed as I speak to you now. But Mr. Peck is here with me and I'm sure he'll be very happy to attend to the matter for you."

"By all means," Bill Peck hastened to assure the general manager. "Who does Mr. Ricks want killed and where will he have the body delivered?"

"Hah-hah! Hah-Hah!" Mr. Skinner had a singularly annoying, mirthless laugh, as if he begrudged himself such an unheard-of indulgence. "Mr. Peck says," he informed Cappy, "that he'll be delighted to attend to the matter for you. He wants to know whom you want killed and where you wish the body delivered. Hah-hah! Hah! Peck, Mr. Ricks will speak to you."

Bill Peck took the telephone. "Good afternoon, Mr. Ricks."

"Hello, old soldier. What are you doing this afternoon?"

"Nothing, after I conclude my conference with Mr. Skinner. By the way, he has just given me a most handsome boost in salary, for which I am most appreciative. I feel, however, despite Mr. Skinner's graciousness, that you have put in a kind word for me with him, and I want to thank you"

"Tut, tut. Not a peep out of you, sir. Not a peep. You get nothing for nothing from Skinner or me. However, in view of the fact that you're feeling kindly toward me this afternoon, I wish you'd do a little errand for me. I can't send a boy and I hate to make a messenger out of you--er--ah--ahem! That is har-umph-h-h--!"

"I have no false pride, Mr. Ricks."

"Thank you, Bill. Glad you feel that way about it. Bill, I was prowling around town this forenoon, after church, and down in a store on Sutter Street, between Stockton and Powell Street, on the right-hand side as you face Market Street, I saw a blue vase in a window. I have a weakness for vases, Bill. I'm a sharp on them, too. Now, this vase I saw isn't very expensive as vases go in fact, I wouldn't buy it for my collection--but one of the finest and sweetest ladies of my acquaintance has the mate to that blue vase I saw in the window, and I know she'd be prouder than Punch if she had two of them, one for each side of her drawing room mantel, understand?

"Now, I'm leaving from the Southern Pacific depot at eight o'clock tonight, bound for Santa Barbara to attend her wedding anniversary tomorrow night. I forget what anniversary it is, Bill, but I have been informed by my daughter that I'll be very much de trop if I send her any present other than something in porcelain or China or Cloisonné well, Bill, this crazy little blue vase just fills the order. Understand?"

"Yes, sir. You feel that it would be most graceful on your part if you could bring this little blue vase down to Santa Barbara with you tonight. You have to have it tonight, because if you wait until the store opens on Monday the vase will reach your hostess twenty-four hours after her anniversary party."

"Exactly, Bill. Now, I've simply got to have that vase. If I had discovered it yesterday, I wouldn't be asking you to get it for me today, Bill."

"Please do not make any explanations or apologies, Mr. Ricks. You have described the vase no you haven't. What sort of blue is it, how tall is it and what is, approximately, its greatest diameter? Does it set on a base, or does it not? Is it a solid blue, or is it figured?"

It's a Cloisonné vase, Bill sort of old Dutch blue, or Delft, with some Oriental funny business on it. I couldn't describe it exactly, but it has some birds and flowers on it. It's about a foot tall and four inches in diameter and sets on a teak-wood base."

"Very well, sir. You shall have it."

"And you'll deliver it to me in stateroom A, car 7, aboard the train at Third and Townsend Streets, at seven fifty-five tonight?"

"Yes, sir."

"Thank you, Bill. The expense will be trifling. Collect it from the cashier in the morning and tell him to charge it to my account." And Cappy hung up.

At once Mr. Skinner took up the thread of the interrupted conference, and it was not until three o'clock that Bill Peck left his house and proceeded downtown to locate Cappy Rick's blue vase.

He proceeded to the block in Sutter Street between Stockton and Powell Streets, and although he walked patiently up one side of the street and down the other, not a single vase of any description showed in any shop window, nor could he find a single shop where such a vase as Cappy had described might, perchance, be displayed for sale.

"I think the old boy has erred in the co-ordinates of the target," Bill Peck concluded, "or else I misunderstood him. I'll telephone his house and ask him to repeat them."

He did, but nobody was at home except a Swedish maid, and all she knew was that Mr. Ricks was out and the hour of his return was unknown. So Mr. Peck went back to Sutter Street and scoured once more every shop window in the block. Then he scouted two blocks above Powell and two blocks below Stockton. Still the blue vase remained invisible.

So, he transferred his search to a corresponding area on Bush Street, and when that failed, he went painstakingly over four blocks of Post Street. He was still without results when he moved one block further west and one further south and discovered the blue vase in a huge plate-glass window of a shop on Geary Street near Grant Avenue. He surveyed it critically and was convinced that it was the object he sought.

He tried the door, but it was locked, as he had anticipated it would be. So, he kicked the door and raised an infernal racket, hoping against hope that the noise might bring a watchman from the rear of the building. In vain. He backed out to the edge of the sidewalk and read the sign over the door:

B. Cohen's Art Shop

This was a start, so Mr. Peck limped over to the Palace Hotel and procured a telephone directory. By actual count there were nineteen B. Cohens scattered throughout the city, so before commencing to call the nineteen, Bill Peck borrowed the city directory from the hotel clerk and scanned it for the particular B. Cohen who owned the art shop. His search availed him nothing. B. Cohen was listed as an art dealer at the address where the blue vase reposed in the show window. That was all.

"I suppose he's a commuter," Mr. Peck concluded, and at once proceeded to procure directories of the adjacent cities of Berkeley, Oakland, and Alameda. They were not available, so in despair he changed a dollar into five cent pieces, sought a telephone booth and commenced calling up all the B. Cohens in San Francisco. Of the nineteen, four did not answer, three were temporarily disconnected, six replied in Yiddish, five were not the B. Cohen he sought, and one swore he was Irish and that his name was spelled Cohan and pronounced with an accent on both syllables.

The B. Cohens resident in Berkeley, Oakland, Alameda, San Rafael, Sausalito, Mill Valley, San Mateo, Redwood City and Palo Alto were next telephoned to, and when this long and expensive task was done, Ex-Private Bill Peck emerged from the telephone booth wringing wet with perspiration and as irritable as a clucking hen. Once outside the hotel he raised his haggard face to heaven and dumbly queried of the Almighty what He meant by saving him from quick death on the field of honour only to condemn him to be talked to death by B. Cohens in civil life.

It was now six o'clock. Suddenly Peck had an inspiration. Was the name spelled Cohen, Cohan, Cohn, Kohn, or Coen?

"If I have to take a Jewish census again tonight, I'll die," he told himself desperately, and went back to the art shop.

The sign read: B. COHN'S ART SHOP.

"I wish I knew a bootlegger's joint," poor Peck complained. "I'm pretty far gone, and a little wood alcohol couldn't hurt me much now. Why, I could have sworn that name was spelled with an E. It seems to me I noted that particularly."

He went back to the hotel telephone booth and commenced calling up all the B. Cohn's in town. There were eight of them and six of them were out, one was maudlin with liquor and the other was very deaf and shouted unintelligibly.

"Peace hath its barbarities no less than war," Mr. Peck sighed. He changed a twenty-dollar bill into nickles, dimes and quarters, returned to the hot, ill-smelling telephone booth and proceeded to lay down a barrage of telephone calls to the B. Cohn's of all towns of any importance contiguous to San Francisco Bay. And he was lucky. On the sixth call he located the particular B. Cohn in San Rafael, only to be informed by Mr. Cohn's cook that Mr. Cohn was dining at the home of a Mr. Simons in Mill Valley.

There were three Mr. Simons in Mill Valley, and Peck called them all before connecting with the right one. Yes, Mr. B. Cohn was there. Who wished to speak to him? Mr. Heck? Oh, Mr. Lake! A silence. Then Mr. Cohn says he doesn't know any Mr. Lake and wants to know the nature of your business. He is dining and doesn't like to be disturbed unless the matter is of grave importance."

"Tell him Mr. Peck wishes to speak to him on a matter of very great importance," wailed the ex-private.

"Mr. Metz? Mr. Ben Metz?

"No, no, no. Peck--p-e-c-k."

"D-e-c-k?"

"No, P."

"C?"

"P."

"Oh, yes, E. E-what?"

"C-K.."

"Oh, yes, Mr. Eckstein."

"Call Cohn to the 'phone or I'll go over there on the next boat and kill you, you damned idiot," shrieked Peck. "Tell him his store is on fire."

That message was evidently delivered for almost instantly Mr. B. Cohn was puffing and spluttering into the phone.

"Is dot der fire marshal?" he managed to articulate.

"Listen, Mr. Cohn. Your store is not on fire, but I had to say so in order to get you to the telephone. I am Mr. Peck, a total stranger to you. You have a blue vase in your shop window on Geary Street in San Francisco. I want to buy it and I want to buy it before seven forty-five tonight. I want you to come across the bay and open the store and sell me that vase."

"Such a business! Vot, you think I am? Crazy?"

"No, Mr. Cohn, I do not. I'm the only crazy man talking. I'm crazy for that vase and I've got to have it right away."

"You know vot dot vase costs?" Mr. B. Cohn's voice dripped syrup.

"No, and I don't give a hoot what it costs. I want what I want when I want it. Do I get it?"

"Ve-ell, let me see. Vot time, is it?" A silence while B. Cohn evidently looked at his watch. "It is now a quarter of seven, Mr. Eckstein, und der next drain from Mill Valley don't leaf until eight o'clock. Dot vill get me to San Francisco at eight-fifty and I am dining mit friends und have just finished my soup."

"To hell with your soup. I want that blue vase."

"Vell, I tell you, Mr. Eckstein, if you got to have it, call up my head salesman, Herman Joost, in der Chilton Apartments Prospect three--two--four--nine, und tell him I said he should come down right away quick and sell you dot blue vase. Goodbye, Mr. Eckstein."

And B. Cohn hung up.

Instantly Peck called Prospect 3249 and asked for Herman Joost. Mr. Joost's mother answered. She was desolated because Herman was not at home but vouchsafed the information that he was dining at the country club. Which country club? She did not know. So, Peck procured from the hotel clerk a list of the country clubs in and around San Francisco and started calling them up. At eight o'clock he was still being informed that Mr. Juice was not a member, that Mr. Luce wasn't in, that Mr. Coos had been dead three months and that Mr. Boos had played but eight holes when he received a telegram calling him back to New York. At the other clubs Mr. Joust was unknown.

"Licked," murmured Bill Peck, "but never let it be said that I didn't go down fighting. I'm going to heave a brick through that show window, grab the vase and run with it."

He engaged a taxicab and instructed the driver to wait for him at the corner of Geary and Stockton Streets. Also, he borrowed from the chauffeur a ball peen hammer. When he reached the art shop of B. Cohn, however, a policeman was standing in the doorway, violating the general orders of a policeman on duty by surreptitiously smoking a cigar.

"He'll nab me if I crack that window," the desperate Peck decided, and continued on down the street, crossed to the other side, and came back. It was now dark and over the art shop B. Cohn's name burned in small red, white, and blue electric lights.

And lo, it was spelled B. Cohen!

Ex-private William E. Peck sat down on a fire hydrant and cursed with rage. His weak leg hurt him, too, and for some damnable reason, the stump of his left arm developed the feeling that his missing hand was itchy.

"The world is filled with idiots," he raved furiously. "I'm tired and I'm hungry. I skipped luncheon and I've been too busy to think of dinner."

He walked back to his taxicab and returned to the hotel where, hope springing eternal in his breast, he called Prospect 3249 again and discovered that the missing Herman Joost had returned to the bosom of his family. To him the frantic Peck delivered the message of B. Cohn, whereupon the cautious Herman Joost replied that he would confirm the authenticity of the message by telephoning to Mr. Cohn at Mr. Simon's home in Mill Valley. If Mr. B. Cohn or Cohen confirmed Mr. Kek's story he, the said Herman Joost, would be at the store sometime before nine o'clock, and if Mr. Kek cared to, he might await him there.

Mr. Kek said he would be delighted to wait for him there.

At nine-fifteen Herman Joost appeared on the scene. On his way down the street, he had taken the precaution to pick up a policeman and bring him along with him. The lights were switched on in the store and Mr. Joost lovingly abstracted the blue vase from the window.

"What's the cursed thing worth?" Peck demanded.

"Two thousand dollars," Mr. Joost replied without so much as the quiver of an eyelash. "Cash," he added, apparently as an afterthought.

The exhausted Peck leaned against the sturdy guardian of the law and sighed. This was the final straw. He had about ten dollars in his possession.

"You refuse, absolutely, to accept my check?" he quavered.

"I don't know you, Mr. Peck," Herman Joost replied simply.

"Where's your telephone?"

Mr. Joost led Peck to the telephone and the latter called up Mr. Skinner.

"Mr. Skinner," he announced, "this is all that is mortal of Bill Peck speaking. I've got the store open and for two thousand dollars cash, I can buy the blue vase Mr. Ricks has set his heart upon."

"Oh, Peck, dear fellow," Mr. Skinner purred sympathetically. "Have you been all this time on that errand?"

"I have. And I'm going to stick on the job until I deliver the goods. For God's sake let me have two thousand dollars and bring it down to me at B. Cohen's Art Shop on Geary Street near Grant Avenue. I'm too utterly exhausted to go up after it."

"My dear Mr. Peck, I haven't two thousand dollars in my house. That is too great a sum of money to keep on hand."

"Well, then, come downtown, open up the office safe and get the money for me."

"Time lock on the office safe, Peck. Impossible."

"Well then, come downtown and identify me at hotels and cafés and restaurants so I can cash my own check."

"Is your check good, Mr. Peck?"

The flood of invective which had been accumulating in Mr. Peck's system all the afternoons now broke its bounds. He screamed at Mr. Skinner a blasphemous invitation to betake himself to the lower regions.

"Tomorrow morning," he promised hoarsely, "I'll beat you to death with the stump of my left arm, you are miserable, cold-blooded, lazy, shiftless slacker."

He called up Cappy Ricks' residence next, and asked for Captain Matt Peasley, who, he knew, made his home with his father-in-law. Matt Peasley came to the telephone and listened sympathetically to Peck's tale of woe.

"Peck, that's the worst outrage I ever heard of," he declared. "The idea of setting you such a task. You take my advice and forget the blue vase."

"I can't," Peck panted. "Mr. Ricks will feel mighty chagrined if I fail to get the vase to him. I would not disappoint him for my right arm. He's been a dead game sport with me, Captain Peasley."

"But it's too late to get the vase to him, Peck. He left the city at eight o'clock and it is now almost half past nine."

"I know, but if I can secure legal possession of the vase, I'll get it to him before he leaves the train at Santa Barbara at six o'clock tomorrow morning."

"How?"

"There's a flying school out at the Marina and one of the pilots there is a friend of mine. He'll fly to Santa Barbara with me and the vase."

"You're crazy."

"I know it. Please lend me two thousand dollars."

"What for?"

"To pay for the vase."

"Now I know you're crazy or drunk. Why if Cappy Ricks ever forgot himself to the extent of paying two hundred dollars for a vase he'd bleed to death in an hour."

"Won't you let me have two thousand dollars, Captain Peasley?"

"I will not, Peck, old son. Go home and to bed and forget it."

"Please. You can cash your checks. You are known so much better than I, and it's Sunday night--"

"And it's a fine way to keep holy the Sabbath day," Matt Peasley retorted and hung up.

"Well," Herman Joost queried, "do we stay here all night?"

Bill Peck bowed his head. "Look here," he demanded suddenly, "do you know a good diamond when you see it?"

"I do," Herman Joost replied.

"Will you wait here until I go to my hotel and get one?"

"Sure."

Bill Peck limped painfully away. Forty minutes later he returned with a platinum ring set with diamonds and sapphires.

"What are they worth?" he demanded.

Herman Joost looked the ring over lovingly and appraised it conservatively at twenty-five hundred dollars.

"Take it as security for the payment of my check," Peck pleaded. "Give me a receipt for it and after my check has gone through clearing, I'll come back and get the ring."

Fifteen minutes later, with the blue vase packed in excelsior and reposing in a stout cardboard box, Bill Peck entered a restaurant and ordered dinner. When he had dined, he engaged a taxi and was driven to the flying field at the Marina. From the night watchman he ascertained the address of his pilot friend and at midnight, with his friend at the wheel, Bill Peck and his blue vase soared up into the moonlight and headed south.

An hour and a half later they landed in a stubble field in the Salinas Valley and, bidding his friend good-bye, Bill Peck trudged across to the railroad track and sat down. When the train bearing Cappy Ricks came roaring down the valley, Peck twisted a Sunday paper with which he had provided himself, into an improvised torch, which he lighted. Standing between the rails he swung the flaming paper frantically.

The train slid to a halt, a brakeman opened a vestibule door, and Bill Peck stepped wearily aboard.

"What do you mean by flagging this train?" the brakeman demanded angrily, as he signalled the engineer to proceed. "Got a ticket?"

"No, but I've got the money to pay my way. And I flagged this train because I wanted to change my method of travel. I'm looking for a man in stateroom A of car 7, and if you try to block me there'll be murder done."

"That's right. Take advantage of your half-portion arm and abuse me," the brakeman retorted bitterly. "Are you looking for that little old man with the Henry Clay collar and the white mutton-chop whiskers?"

"I certainly am."

"Well, he was looking for you just before we left San Francisco. He asked me if I had seen a one-armed man with a box under his good arm. I'll lead you to him."

A prolonged ringing at Cappy's stateroom door brought the old gentleman to the entrance in his nightshirt.

"Very sorry to have to disturb you, Mr. Ricks," said Bill Peck, "but the fact is there were so many Cohens and Cohns and Cohans, and it was such a job to dig up two thousand dollars, that I failed to connect with you at seven forty-five last night, as per orders. It was absolutely impossible for me to accomplish the task within the time limit set, but I was resolved that you should not be disappointed. Here is the vase. The shop wasn't within four blocks of where you thought it was, sir, but I'm sure I found the right vase. It ought to be. It cost enough and was hard enough to get, so it should be precious enough to form a gift for any friend of yours."

Cappy Ricks stared at Bill Peck as if the latter were a wraith.

"By the Twelve Ragged Apostles!" he murmured. "By the Holy Pink-toed Prophet! We changed the sign on you and we stacked the Cohens on you and we set a policeman to guard the shop to keep you from breaking the window, and we made you dig up two thousand dollars on Sunday night in a town where you are practically unknown, and while you missed the train at eight o'clock, you overtake it at two o'clock in the morning and deliver the blue vase. Come in and rest your poor old game leg, Bill. Brake-man, I'm much obliged to you."

Bill Peck entered and slumped wearily down on the settee. "So, it was a plant?" he cracked, and his voice trembled with rage. "Well, sir, you're an old man and you've been good to me, so I do not begrudge you your little joke, but Mr. Ricks, I can't stand things like I used to. My leg hurts and my stump hurts and my heart hurts------"

He paused, choking, and the tears of impotent rage filled his eyes. "You shouldn't treat me that way, sir," he complained presently. "I've been trained not to question orders, even when they seem utterly foolish to me; I've been trained to obey them on time, if possible, but if impossible, to obey them anyhow. I've been taught loyalty to my chief and I'm sorry my chief found it necessary to make a buffoon of me. I haven't had a very good time the past three years and--and--you can--pa-pa-pass your skunk spruce and larch rustic and short, odd length stock to some slacker like Skinner and you'd better arrange to replace Skinner, because he's young enough to take a beating and I'm going to give it to him, and it'll be a hospital job sir"

Cappy Ricks ruffled Bill Peck's aching head with a paternal hand.

"Bill, old boy, it was cruel damnably cruel, but I had a big job for you, and I had to find out a lot of things about you before I entrusted you with that job. So, I arranged to give you the Degree of the Blue Vase, which is the supreme test of a go-getter. You thought you carried into this stateroom a two-thousand-dollar vase, but between ourselves, what you really carried in was a ten-thousand-dollar job as our

Shanghai manager."

"Wha..what!"

"Every time I have to pick out a permanent holder of a job worth ten thousand dollars, or more, I give the candidate the Degree of the Blue Vase," Cappy explained. "I've had two men out of a field of fifteen deliver the vase, Bill."

Bill Peck had forgotten his rage, but the tears of his recent fury still glistened in his bold blue eyes. "Thank you, sir. I forgive you and I'll make good in Shanghai."

"I know you will, Bill. Now, tell me, son, weren't you tempted to quit when you discovered the almost insuperable obstacles I'd placed in your way?"

"Yes, sir, I was. I wanted to commit suicide before I'd finished telephoning all the C-o-h-e-n-s in the world. And when I started on the C-o-h-n-s--well, it's this way, sir. I just couldn't quit because that would have been disloyal to a man I once knew."

"Who was he?" Cappy demanded, and there was awe in his voice.

"He was my brigadier, and he had a brigade motto: It shall be done. When the divisional commander called him up and told him to move forward with his brigade and occupy certain territory, our brigadier would say: 'Very well, sir. It shall be done.' If any officer in his brigade showed signs of flunking his job because it appeared impossible, the brigadier would just look at him once and then that officer would remember the motto and go and do his job or die trying.

"In the army, sir, the esprit de corps doesn't bubble up from the bottom. It filters down from the top. An organization is what its commanding officer is neither better nor worse. In my company, when the top sergeant handed out a week of kitchen police to a buck, that buck was out of luck if he couldn't muster a grin and say: 'All right, sergeant. It shall be done.'

"The brigadier sent for me once and ordered me to go out and get a certain German sniper. I'd been pretty lucky some days I got enough for a mess, and he'd heard of me. He opened a map and said to me: 'Here's about where he holes up. Go get him, Private Peck.' Well, Mr. Ricks, I snapped into it and gave him a rifle salute, and said, 'Sir, it shall be done' and I'll never forget the look that man gave me. He came down to the field hospital to see me after I'd walked into one of those Austrian 88's. I knew my left wing was a total loss and I suspected my left leg was about to leave me, and I was downhearted and wanted to die. He came and bucked me up. He said: 'Why, Private Peck, you aren't half dead. In civil life you're going to be worth half a dozen live ones, aren't you?' But I was pretty far gone, and I told him I didn't believe it, so he gave me a hard look and said: 'Private Peck will do his utmost to recover and as a starter he will smile.' Of course, putting it in the form of an order, I had to give him the usual reply, so I grinned and said: 'Sir, it shall be done.' He was quite a man, sir, and his brigade had a soul, his soul"

"I see, Bill. And his soul goes marching on, eh? Who was he, Bill?"

Bill Peck named his idol.

"By the Twelve Ragged Apostles!" There was awe in Cappy Ricks' voice, there was reverence in his faded old eyes. "Son," he continued gently, "twenty-five years ago your brigadier was a candidate for an important job in my employ and I gave him the Degree of the Blue Vase. He couldn't get the vase legitimately, so he threw a cobblestone through the window, grabbed the vase, and ran a mile and a half before the police captured him. Cost me a lot of money to square the case and keep it quiet. But he was too good, Bill, and I couldn't stand in his way; I let him go forward to his destiny. But tell me, Bill. How did you get the two thousand dollars to pay for this vase?"

"Once," said ex-Private Peck thoughtfully, "the brigadier and I were first at a dug-out entrance. It was a headquarters dug-out and they wouldn't surrender, so I bombed them and then we went down. I found a finger with a ring on it--and the brigadier said if I didn't take the ring somebody else would. I left that ring as security for my check."

"But how could you have the courage to let me in for a two-thousand-dollar vase? Didn't you realize that the price was absurd and that I might repudiate the transaction?"

"Certainly not. You are responsible for the acts of your servant. You are a true-blue sport and would never repudiate my action. You told me what to do, but you did not insult my intelligence by telling me how to do it. When my late brigadier sent me after the German sniper, he didn't take into consideration the probability that the sniper might get me. He told me to get the sniper. It was my business to see to it that I accomplished my mission and carried my objective, which, of course, I could not have done if I had permitted the German to get me."

"I see, Bill. Well, give that blue vase to the porter in the morning. I paid fifteen cents for it in a five, ten and fifteen cent stores. Meanwhile, hop into that upper berth and help yourself to a well-earned rest."

"But aren't you going to a wedding anniversary at Santa Barbara, Mr. Ricks?"

"I am not. Bill, I discovered a long time ago that it's a good idea for me to get out of town and play golf as often as I can. Besides which, prudence dictates that I remain away from the office for a week after the seeker of blue vases fails to deliver the goods and by the way, Bill, what sort of a game do you play? Oh, forgive me, Bill. I forgot about your left arm."

"Say, look here, sir," Bill Peck retorted, "I'm big enough and ugly enough to play one-handed golf."

"But have you ever tried it?"

"No, sir," Bill Peck replied seriously, "but it shall be done!"

LIST OF TITLES WITH ISBN NO.

ISBN	TITLE
9788194914129	1984
9789390575220	1984 & Animal Farm (2In1)
9789390575572	1984 & Animal Farm (2In1): The International Best-Selling Classics
9789390575848	35 Sonnets
9789390575329	A Clergyman's Daughter
9789390575923	A Study In Scarlet
9789390896097	A Tale Of Two Cities
9789390896837	Abide in Christ
9789390896202	Abraham Lincoln
9789390896912	Absolute Surrender
9789390896608	African American Classic Collection
9789390575305	Aldous Huxley: The Collected Works
9789390896141	An Autobiography of M. K. Gandhi
9789390575886	Animal Farm
9789390575619	Animal Farm & The Great Gatsby (2In1)
9789390575626	Animal Farm & We
9789390896158	Anna Karenina
9789390575534	Antic Hay
9789390896165	Antony & Cleopatra
9789390896172	As I Lay Dying
9789390896226	As You like it
9789390575671	At Your Command
9789390575350	Awakened Imagination
9789390575114	Be What You Wish
9789390896233	Believe In yourself
9789390896998	Best of Charles Darwin: The Origin of Species & Autobiography
9789390896684	Best Of Horror : Dracula And Frankenstein
9789390575503	Best Of Mark Twain (The Adventures of Tom Sawyer AND The Adventures of Huckleberry Finn)
9789390896769	Black History Collection
9789390575756	Brave New World, Animal Farm & 1984 (3in1)

9789390896240	Brother Karamzov
9789390575053	Bulleh Shah Poetry
9789390575725	Burmese Days
9789390896257	Bushido
9789390896066	Can't Hurt Me
9788194914112	Chanakya Neeti: With The Complete Sutras
9789390896042	Crime and Punishment
9789390575527	Crome Yellow
9789390575046	Down and Out in Paris and London
9789390896844	Dracula
9789390575442	Emersons Essays: The Complete First & Second Series (Self-Reliance & Other Essays)
9789390575749	Emma
9789390575817	Essential Tozer Collection - The Pursuit of God & The Purpose of Man
9789390896578	Fascism What It Is and How to Fight It
9789390575688	Feeling is the Secret
9789390575190	Five Lessons
9789390575954	Frankenstein
9789390575237	Franz Kafka: Collected Works
9789390575282	Franz Kafka: Short Stories
9789390575060	George Orwell Collected Works
9789390575077	George Orwell Essays
9789390575213	George Orwell Poems
9788194914150	Greatest Poetry Ever Written Vol 1
9788194914143	Greatest Poetry Ever Written Vol 1
9789390896301	Gulliver's Travel
9789390575961	Gunaho Ka Devta
9789390575893	H. P. Lovecraft Selected Stories Vol 1
9789390575978	H. P. Lovecraft Selected Stories Vol 2
9789390896059	Hamlet
9789390575022	His Last Bow: Some Reminiscences of Sherlock Holmes
9789390896134	History of Western Philosophy
9789390575121	Homage To Catalonia

9789390896219	How to develop self-confidence and Improve public Speaking
9789390896295	How to enjoy your life and your Job
9789390575633	How to own your own mind
9789390896318	How to read Human Nature
9789390896325	How to sell your way through the life
9789390896370	How to use the laws of mind
9789390896387	How to use the power of prayer
9789390896028	How to win friends & Influence People
9788194824176	How To Win Friends and Influence People
9789390896103	Humility The Beauty of Holiness
9789390896653	Imperialism the Highest Stage of Capitalism
9789390575084	In Our Time
9789390575169	In Our Time & Three Stories and Ten poems
9789390575145	James Allen: The Collected Works
9789390896189	Jesus Himself
9789390575480	Jo's Boys
9789390896394	Julius Caesar
9789390575404	Keep the Aspidistra Flying
9789390896400	Kidnapped
9789390896424	King Lear
9789390575824	Lady Susan
9789390896455	Law of Success
9789390896264	Lincoln The Unknown
9789390575565	Little Men
9789390575640	Little Women
9788194914174	Lost Horizon
9789390896462	Macbeth
9789390896929	Man Eaters of Kumaon
9789390896523	Man The Dwelling Place of God
9789390896349	Man The Dwelling Place of God
9789390575909	Mansfield Park
9788194914136	Manto Ki 25 Sarvshreshth Kahaniya
9789390896509	Marxism, Anarchism, Communism
9789390575664	Mathematical Principles of Natural Philosophy

9788194914198	Meditations
9789390575800	Mein Kampf
9789390575794	Memory How To Develop, Train, And Use It
9789390896486	Mind Power
9789390896585	Money
9789390575039	Mortal Coils
9789390575770	My Life and Work
9789390896035	Narrative of the Life of Frederick Douglass
9789390575152	Neville Goddard: The Collected Works
9789390575985	Northanger Abbey
9789390896530	Notes From Underground
9789390896547	Oliver Twist
9789390575459	On War
9789390575541	One, None and a Hundred Thousand
9789390896554	Othelo
9789390575435	Out Of This World
9789390575015	Persuasion
9789390575510	Prayer The Art Of Believing
9789390575091	Pride and Prejudice
9789390896561	Psychic Perception
9789390575381	Rabindranath Tagore - 5 Best Short Stories Vol 2
9789390575367	Rabindranath Tagore - Short Stories (Masters Collections Including The Childs Return)
9789390575374	Rabindranath Tagore 5 Best Short Stories Vol 1 (Including The Childs Return
9789390896622	Romeo & Juliet
9789390896127	Sanatana Dharma
9789390575596	Seedtime & Harvest
9789390896639	Selected Stories of Guy De Maupassant
9789390575206	Self-Reliance & Other Essays
9789390575176	Sense and Sensibility
9789390575299	Shyamchi Aai
9789390896738	Socialism Utopian and Scientific
9789390896646	Success Through a Positive Mental Attitude
9789390575428	The Adventures of Huckleberry Finn

9789390575183	The Adventures of Sherlock Holmes
9789390575343	The Adventures of Tom Sawyer
9789390896691	The Alchemy Of Happiness
9789390575862	The Art Of Public Speaking
9789390896288	The Autobiography Of Charles Darwin
9788194914181	The Best of Franz Kafka: The Metamorphosis & The Trial
9789390575008	The Call Of Cthulhu and Other Weird Tales
9789390575107	The Case-Book of Sherlock Holmes
9789390896110	The Castle Of Otranto
9789390896745	The Communist Manifesto
9789390575589	The Complete Fiction of H. P. Lovecraft
9789390575497	The Complete Works of Florence Scovel Shinn
9789390896820	The Conquest of Breard
9789390896813	The Diary of a Young Girl
9789390896332	The Diary of a Young Girl The Definitive Edition of the Worlds Most Famous Diary
9789390575701	The Great Gatsby, Animal Farm & 1984 (3In1)
9789390575312	The Greatest Works Of George Orwell (5 Books) Including 1984 & Non-Fiction
9789390575992	The Hound of Baskervilles
9789390896707	The Idiot
9789390896714	The Invisible Man
9789390575657	The Knowledge of the holy
9789390575558	The Law & the Promise
9789390896721	The Law Of Attraction
9789390896776	The Leader in you
9789390896363	The Life of Christ
9789390896196	The Man-Eating Leopard of Rudraprayag
9789390896783	The Master Key to Riches
9789390575268	The Memoirs Of Sherlock Holmes
9789390896479	The Midsummer Night's Dream
9789390575466	The Mill On The Floss
9789390896790	The Miracles of your mind
9789390896660	The Mutual Aid A Factor in Evolution
9789390896448	The Origin of Species

9789390896905	The Peter Kropotkin Anthology The Conquest of Bread & Mutual Aid A Factor of Evolution
9789390896806	The Picture of Dorian Gray
9789390896271	The Picture of Dorian Gray
9789390575275	The Power Of Awareness
9789390896356	The Power of Concentration
9788194824169	The Power of Positive Thinking
9789390575411	The Power of the Spoken Word
9788194914105	The Power Of Your Subconscious Mind
9789390896899	The Power of Your Subconscious Mind
9789390896417	The Principles of Communism
9789390575787	The Psychology Of Mans Possible Evolution
9789390896615	The Psychology of Salesmanship
9789390575732	The Pursuit of God
9789390575398	The Pursuit of Happiness
9789390896851	The Quick and Easy Way to effective Speaking
9789390575947	The Return Of Sherlock Holmes
9789390575138	The Road To Wigan Pier
9789390896981	The Root of the Righteous
9789390575855	The Science Of Being Well
9788194914167	The Science Of Getting Rich, The Science Of Being Great & The Science Of Being Well (3In1)
9789390896011	The Screwtape Letters
9789390896073	The Screwtape Letters
9789390575336	The Secret Door to Success
9789390575695	The Secret Of Imagining
9789390896868	The Secret Of Success
9789390896431	The Seven Last Words
9789390575930	The Sign of the Four
9789390896004	The Sonnets
9789390896516	The Souls of Black Folk
9789390896875	The Sound and The Fury
9789390575244	The State and Revolution
9789390896882	The Story of My Life
9789390896936	The Story Of Oriental Philosophy

9789390896752	The Strange Case of Dr. Jekyll and Mr. Hyde
9789390896943	The Tempest
9789390575916	The Valley Of Fear
9789390575879	The Wind in the willows
9789390896080	The Wind in the willows
9789390575763	Their eyes were watching gofd
9789390575831	Three Stories
9789390896950	Twelfth Night
9789390896592	Twelve Years a Slave
9789390896677	Up from Slavery
9789390896974	Value Price and Profit
9789390896967	Wake Up and Live
9789390896493	With Christ in the School of Prayer
9789390575602	Your Faith is Your Fortune
9789390575473	Your Infinite Power To Be Rich
9789390575251	Your Word is Your Wand
9789390575718	Youth
9789391316099	A Christmas Carol
9789391316105	A Doll's House
9789391316501	A Passage to India
9789391316709	A Portrait of the Artist as a Young Man
9789391316112	A Tale of Two Cities
9789391316747	A Tear and a Smile
9789391316167	Agnes Gray
9789391316174	Alice's Adventures in Wonderland
9789391316136	Anandamath
9789391316181	Anne Of Green Gables
9789391316754	Anthem
9789391316198	Around The World in 80 Days
9789391316013	As A Man Thinketh
9789391316242	Autobiography of a Yogi
9789391316266	Beyond Good and Evil
9789391316761	Bleak House
9789391316778	Chitra, a Play in One Act
9789391316310	David Copperfield

9789391316075	Demian
9789391316785	Dubliners
9789391316051	Favourite Tales from the Arabian Nights
9789391316235	Gitanjali
9789391316068	Gravity
9789391316150	Great Speeches of Abraham Lincoln
9789391316662	Guerilla Warfare
9789391316839	Kim
9789391316822	Mother
9789391316211	My Childhood
9789391316846	Nationalism
9789391316327	Oliver Twist
9789391316853	Pygmalion
9789391316334	Relativity: The Special and the General Theory
9789391316389	Scientific Healing Affirmation
9789391316341	Sons and Lovers
9789391316587	Tales from India
9789391316372	Tess of The D'Urbervilles
9789391316396	The Awakening and Selected Stories
9789391316402	The Bhagvad Gita
9789391316303	The Book of Enoch
9789391316228	The Canterville Ghost
9789391316907	The Dynamic Laws of Prosperity
9789391316006	The Great Gatsby
9789391316860	The Hungry Stones and Other Stories
9789391316433	The Idiot
9789391316440	The Importance of Being Earnest
9789391316297	The Light of Asia
9789391316914	The Madman His Parables and Poems
9789391316457	The Odyssey
9789391316921	The Picture of Dorian Gray
9789391316464	The Prince
9789391316938	The Prophet
9789391316945	The Republic
9789391316518	The Scarlet Letter

9789391316143	The Seven Laws of Teaching
9789391316525	The Story of My Experiments with Truth
9789391316532	The Tales of the Mother Goose
9789391316549	The Thirty Nine Steps
9789391316594	The Time Machine
9789391316600	The Turn of the Screw
9789391316983	The Upanishads
9789391316617	The Yellow Wallpaper
9789391316426	The Yoga Sutras of Patanjali
9789391316990	Ulysses
9789391316624	Utopia
9789391316679	Vanity Fair
9789391316020	What Is To Be Done
9789391316686	Within A Budding Grove
9789391316693	Women in Love

LIST OF TITLES WITH ISBN NO.

ISBN	TITLE
9788194914129	1984
9789390575220	1984 & Animal Farm (2In1)
9789390575572	1984 & Animal Farm (2In1): The International Best-Selling Classics
9789390575848	35 Sonnets
9789390575329	A Clergyman's Daughter
9789390575923	A Study In Scarlet
9789390896097	A Tale Of Two Cities
9789390896837	Abide in Christ
9789390896202	Abraham Lincoln
9789390896912	Absolute Surrender
9789390896608	African American Classic Collection
9789390575305	Aldous Huxley: The Collected Works
9789390896141	An Autobiography of M. K. Gandhi
9789390575886	Animal Farm
9789390575619	Animal Farm & The Great Gatsby (2In1)
9789390575626	Animal Farm & We
9789390896158	Anna Karenina
9789390575534	Antic Hay
9789390896165	Antony & Cleopatra
9789390896172	As I Lay Dying
9789390896226	As You like it
9789390575671	At Your Command
9789390575350	Awakened Imagination
9789390575114	Be What You Wish
9789390896233	Believe In yourself
9789390896998	Best of Charles Darwin: The Origin of Species & Autobiography
9789390896684	Best Of Horror : Dracula And Frankenstein
9789390575503	Best Of Mark Twain (The Adventures of Tom Sawyer AND The Adventures of Huckleberry Finn)
9789390896769	Black History Collection
9789390575756	Brave New World, Animal Farm & 1984 (3in1)

9789390896240	Brother Karamzov
9789390575053	Bulleh Shah Poetry
9789390575725	Burmese Days
9789390896257	Bushido
9789390896066	Can't Hurt Me
9788194914112	Chanakya Neeti: With The Complete Sutras
9789390896042	Crime and Punishment
9789390575527	Crome Yellow
9789390575046	Down and Out in Paris and London
9789390896844	Dracula
9789390575442	Emersons Essays: The Complete First & Second Series (Self-Reliance & Other Essays)
9789390575749	Emma
9789390575817	Essential Tozer Collection - The Pursuit of God & The Purpose of Man
9789390896578	Fascism What It Is and How to Fight It
9789390575688	Feeling is the Secret
9789390575190	Five Lessons
9789390575954	Frankenstein
9789390575237	Franz Kafka: Collected Works
9789390575282	Franz Kafka: Short Stories
9789390575060	George Orwell Collected Works
9789390575077	George Orwell Essays
9789390575213	George Orwell Poems
9788194914150	Greatest Poetry Ever Written Vol 1
9788194914143	Greatest Poetry Ever Written Vol 1
9789390896301	Gulliver's Travel
9789390575961	Gunaho Ka Devta
9789390575893	H. P. Lovecraft Selected Stories Vol 1
9789390575978	H. P. Lovecraft Selected Stories Vol 2
9789390896059	Hamlet
9789390575022	His Last Bow: Some Reminiscences of Sherlock Holmes
9789390896134	History of Western Philosophy
9789390575121	Homage To Catalonia

9789390896219	How to develop self-confidence and Improve public Speaking
9789390896295	How to enjoy your life and your Job
9789390575633	How to own your own mind
9789390896318	How to read Human Nature
9789390896325	How to sell your way through the life
9789390896370	How to use the laws of mind
9789390896387	How to use the power of prayer
9789390896028	How to win friends & Influence People
9788194824176	How To Win Friends and Influence People
9789390896103	Humility The Beauty of Holiness
9789390896653	Imperialism the Highest Stage of Capitalism
9789390575084	In Our Time
9789390575169	In Our Time & Three Stories and Ten poems
9789390575145	James Allen: The Collected Works
9789390896189	Jesus Himself
9789390575480	Jo's Boys
9789390896394	Julius Caesar
9789390575404	Keep the Aspidistra Flying
9789390896400	Kidnapped
9789390896424	King Lear
9789390575824	Lady Susan
9789390896455	Law of Success
9789390896264	Lincoln The Unknown
9789390575565	Little Men
9789390575640	Little Women
9788194914174	Lost Horizon
9789390896462	Macbeth
9789390896929	Man Eaters of Kumaon
9789390896523	Man The Dwelling Place of God
9789390896349	Man The Dwelling Place of God
9789390575909	Mansfield Park
9788194914136	Manto Ki 25 Sarvshreshth Kahaniya
9789390896509	Marxism, Anarchism, Communism
9789390575664	Mathematical Principles of Natural Philosophy

9788194914198	Meditations
9789390575800	Mein Kampf
9789390575794	Memory How To Develop, Train, And Use It
9789390896486	Mind Power
9789390896585	Money
9789390575039	Mortal Coils
9789390575770	My Life and Work
9789390896035	Narrative of the Life of Frederick Douglass
9789390575152	Neville Goddard: The Collected Works
9789390575985	Northanger Abbey
9789390896530	Notes From Underground
9789390896547	Oliver Twist
9789390575459	On War
9789390575541	One, None and a Hundred Thousand
9789390896554	Othelo
9789390575435	Out Of This World
9789390575015	Persuasion
9789390575510	Prayer The Art Of Believing
9789390575091	Pride and Prejudice
9789390896561	Psychic Perception
9789390575381	Rabindranath Tagore - 5 Best Short Stories Vol 2
9789390575367	Rabindranath Tagore - Short Stories (Masters Collections Including The Childs Return)
9789390575374	Rabindranath Tagore 5 Best Short Stories Vol 1 (Including The Childs Return
9789390896622	Romeo & Juliet
9789390896127	Sanatana Dharma
9789390575596	Seedtime & Harvest
9789390896639	Selected Stories of Guy De Maupassant
9789390575206	Self-Reliance & Other Essays
9789390575176	Sense and Sensibility
9789390575299	Shyamchi Aai
9789390896738	Socialism Utopian and Scientific
9789390896646	Success Through a Positive Mental Attitude
9789390575428	The Adventures of Huckleberry Finn

9789390575183	The Adventures of Sherlock Holmes
9789390575343	The Adventures of Tom Sawyer
9789390896691	The Alchemy Of Happiness
9789390575862	The Art Of Public Speaking
9789390896288	The Autobiography Of Charles Darwin
9788194914181	The Best of Franz Kafka: The Metamorphosis & The Trial
9789390575008	The Call Of Cthulhu and Other Weird Tales
9789390575107	The Case-Book of Sherlock Holmes
9789390896110	The Castle Of Otranto
9789390896745	The Communist Manifesto
9789390575589	The Complete Fiction of H. P. Lovecraft
9789390575497	The Complete Works of Florence Scovel Shinn
9789390896820	The Conquest of Breard
9789390896813	The Diary of a Young Girl
9789390896332	The Diary of a Young Girl The Definitive Edition of the Worlds Most Famous Diary
9789390575701	The Great Gatsby, Animal Farm & 1984 (3In1)
9789390575312	The Greatest Works Of George Orwell (5 Books) Including 1984 & Non-Fiction
9789390575992	The Hound of Baskervilles
9789390896707	The Idiot
9789390896714	The Invisible Man
9789390575657	The Knowledge of the holy
9789390575558	The Law & the Promise
9789390896721	The Law Of Attraction
9789390896776	The Leader in you
9789390896363	The Life of Christ
9789390896196	The Man-Eating Leopard of Rudraprayag
9789390896783	The Master Key to Riches
9789390575268	The Memoirs Of Sherlock Holmes
9789390896479	The Midsummer Night's Dream
9789390575466	The Mill On The Floss
9789390896790	The Miracles of your mind
9789390896660	The Mutual Aid A Factor in Evolution
9789390896448	The Origin of Species

9789390896905	The Peter Kropotkin Anthology The Conquest of Bread & Mutual Aid A Factor of Evolution
9789390896806	The Picture of Dorian Gray
9789390896271	The Picture of Dorian Gray
9789390575275	The Power Of Awareness
9789390896356	The Power of Concentration
9788194824169	The Power of Positive Thinking
9789390575411	The Power of the Spoken Word
9788194914105	The Power Of Your Subconscious Mind
9789390896899	The Power of Your Subconscious Mind
9789390896417	The Principles of Communism
9789390575787	The Psychology Of Mans Possible Evolution
9789390896615	The Psychology of Salesmanship
9789390575732	The Pursuit of God
9789390575398	The Pursuit of Happiness
9789390896851	The Quick and Easy Way to effective Speaking
9789390575947	The Return Of Sherlock Holmes
9789390575138	The Road To Wigan Pier
9789390896981	The Root of the Righteous
9789390575855	The Science Of Being Well
9788194914167	The Science Of Getting Rich, The Science Of Being Great & The Science Of Being Well (3In1)
9789390896011	The Screwtape Letters
9789390896073	The Screwtape Letters
9789390575336	The Secret Door to Success
9789390575695	The Secret Of Imagining
9789390896868	The Secret Of Success
9789390896431	The Seven Last Words
9789390575930	The Sign of the Four
9789390896004	The Sonnets
9789390896516	The Souls of Black Folk
9789390896875	The Sound and The Fury
9789390575244	The State and Revolution
9789390896882	The Story of My Life
9789390896936	The Story Of Oriental Philosophy

9789390896752	The Strange Case of Dr. Jekyll and Mr. Hyde
9789390896943	The Tempest
9789390575916	The Valley Of Fear
9789390575879	The Wind in the willows
9789390896080	The Wind in the willows
9789390575763	Their eyes were watching gofd
9789390575831	Three Stories
9789390896950	Twelfth Night
9789390896592	Twelve Years a Slave
9789390896677	Up from Slavery
9789390896974	Value Price and Profit
9789390896967	Wake Up and Live
9789390896493	With Christ in the School of Prayer
9789390575602	Your Faith is Your Fortune
9789390575473	Your Infinite Power To Be Rich
9789390575251	Your Word is Your Wand
9789390575718	Youth
9789391316099	A Christmas Carol
9789391316105	A Doll's House
9789391316501	A Passage to India
9789391316709	A Portrait of the Artist as a Young Man
9789391316112	A Tale of Two Cities
9789391316747	A Tear and a Smile
9789391316167	Agnes Gray
9789391316174	Alice's Adventures in Wonderland
9789391316136	Anandamath
9789391316181	Anne Of Green Gables
9789391316754	Anthem
9789391316198	Around The World in 80 Days
9789391316013	As A Man Thinketh
9789391316242	Autobiography of a Yogi
9789391316266	Beyond Good and Evil
9789391316761	Bleak House
9789391316778	Chitra, a Play in One Act
9789391316310	David Copperfield

9789391316075	Demian
9789391316785	Dubliners
9789391316051	Favourite Tales from the Arabian Nights
9789391316235	Gitanjali
9789391316068	Gravity
9789391316150	Great Speeches of Abraham Lincoln
9789391316662	Guerilla Warfare
9789391316839	Kim
9789391316822	Mother
9789391316211	My Childhood
9789391316846	Nationalism
9789391316327	Oliver Twist
9789391316853	Pygmalion
9789391316334	Relativity: The Special and the General Theory
9789391316389	Scientific Healing Affirmation
9789391316341	Sons and Lovers
9789391316587	Tales from India
9789391316372	Tess of The D'Urbervilles
9789391316396	The Awakening and Selected Stories
9789391316402	The Bhagvad Gita
9789391316303	The Book of Enoch
9789391316228	The Canterville Ghost
9789391316907	The Dynamic Laws of Prosperity
9789391316006	The Great Gatsby
9789391316860	The Hungry Stones and Other Stories
9789391316433	The Idiot
9789391316440	The Importance of Being Earnest
9789391316297	The Light of Asia
9789391316914	The Madman His Parables and Poems
9789391316457	The Odyssey
9789391316921	The Picture of Dorian Gray
9789391316464	The Prince
9789391316938	The Prophet
9789391316945	The Republic
9789391316518	The Scarlet Letter

9789391316143	The Seven Laws of Teaching
9789391316525	The Story of My Experiments with Truth
9789391316532	The Tales of the Mother Goose
9789391316549	The Thirty Nine Steps
9789391316594	The Time Machine
9789391316600	The Turn of the Screw
9789391316983	The Upanishads
9789391316617	The Yellow Wallpaper
9789391316426	The Yoga Sutras of Patanjali
9789391316990	Ulysses
9789391316624	Utopia
9789391316679	Vanity Fair
9789391316020	What Is To Be Done
9789391316686	Within A Budding Grove
9789391316693	Women in Love